Expressions of God

By: Gloria J. Malone

Foreword by: Pastor Carlton Bond

Edited by: Kaylee Overbey

BK Royston Publishing LLC

Jeffersonville, IN

BK Royston Publishing
P. O. Box 4321
Jeffersonville, IN 47131
502-802-5385
http://bkroystonpublishing.com
bkroystonpublishing@gmail.com

© Copyright – 2015

All Rights Reserved. No part of this book may be reproduced, stored in a retrieval system, or transmitted by any means without the written permission of the author.

Published by: BK Royston Publishing LLC
Cover photo licensed by: Fotolia.com
Layout: BK Royston Publishing LLC

ISBN 13: 978-0692548875
ISBN-10: 0692548874

Printed in the United States of America

Foreword

Expressions of God is such a fitting title for this beautiful work penned by Sister Gloria Malone. Her words give readers a glimpse into the chapters of her life and create vivid scenes of God's handiwork in nature. As one of the founding members of Right Now Harvest Church, I thank God for her many years of commitment in service and consider it an honor to introduce the world to the treasure that has been released from within her. Anyone that knows this woman of God is fully aware that she loves her heavenly Father, family, and church fellowship without question. If you've not met Sister Gloria, then you are in for a treat as you encounter her heart on the pages of this book. As you read on, enjoy the sweetness and humility of this great woman of faith, which is sure to bless both children and adults. Sister Gloria's faith in Jesus has brought her to this manifestation of God's goodness and will continue to propel her forward into all He has orchestrated in her life.

Pastor Carlton Bond
Right Now Harvest Church
Louisville, Kentucky

Acknowledgement

First, I want to thank my heavenly Father who makes all things possible.

Thank you Pastor Carlton & Co-Pastor Vickie Bond and my Right Now Harvest Church Family, you are all an inspiration to keep my faith in God and continue to express the goodness and love of the Lord to others.

Thank you to my Publisher, BK Royston Publishing, for helping me gather my poems to complete this book.

Ministers Antonio & Sharon Thomas, thank you for your help in making this happen.

To all my children, grandchildren, great-grandchildren and entire family I love you all so much.

Table of Contents

Foreword	
Acknowledgement	
Kitten	1
Butterfly	2
I Have a Snake	3
I Love My Puppy	4
Lord We Are Crying Out to You	5
God I Love You	6
Be for Real – Where are all the Gentlemen?	7
When I Did Not Know	9
Can You Imagine Song The 12 Days of Heaven	10
Thank You God for Making Me	11
Received. I never received a gift like this. Thank you God for Jesus.	13
The Lord Gave Me	14
Dear Jesus I Love You	16
Lord show me Your Way - Song	17
Rain Down On Me – Song	18
Right Now Harvest Church – Examples My Pastors.	19
Through the Good and the Bad	21
The New Life God's Gonna Give ME	22
The 12 Days of Christmas with Jesus	24
A Mother's Christmas Wish – Nothing can Change what it is.	26
Author's Bio	28

Kitten

Hey little Kitten, where have you been?
Have you been running in and out again?

How many little Kittens do I see?
Eight of them and they are quiet as can be.

Kittens are creepy, they love to play.
I see three of them and all of them are gray.

Kittens like to climb, and they scratch everywhere.
They are so soft and cuddly, who wants to play in their hair?

There are big ones, tall ones, and small ones too.
They stay busy and they don't know what to do.

The kittens are eating now soon they will be asleep.
How many of these kittens would you like to keep?

Butterfly

Butterfly, butterfly, high in the sky
Where did you come from and where will you go?

Butterfly, you are so beautiful and have so many colors.
How many like you? There are no others.

Come land on my shoe, I won't run you away.
I don't know that I can say what I will do.

I like to watch you when you fly by.
When you leave, please come back butterfly.

I Have a Snake

I have a snake, and I keep her in the house.
She likes to eat eggs and sometimes a mouse.

She does not move very much,
I have never seen such.

I like to watch her when she opens her eyes.
She moves her head. Sometimes she even plays dead.

Sometimes I pick her up, and she begins to crawl.
Sometimes I put her down, and she curls up in a ball.

I like my snake, she won't cause fright.
Come over and watch her with me. She won't bite.

I Love my Puppy

I love my puppy, do you hear what I say?
My puppy goes with me everywhere. I take him to school because he likes to play.

He likes all my friends. I'm going to keep him until the end.
My puppy lives in my house, he is my best friend.

He likes to play in the leaves with me and he likes to play ball.
My puppy can stand up on his two hind legs, my puppy is not afraid at all.

Oh, I almost forgot
My puppy, his name is Lucky.

Lord We Are Crying Out to You

Lord, we are crying out for the nation, we cry out to you.
Lord, we are crying out for our enemies, we cry out to you.
Lord, we are crying out to you for a change, we cry out to you.
Lord, we are crying for the lost souls, for they must know that you are the answer, we cry out to you.
Lord, hear our prayer right now.
Oh, Lord, the end of time is near,
we cry out to you.
Lord, you are our soon coming King.
Lord, hear our prayer right now,
Lord we are crying out to you. Lord, hear, hear us, Lord, hear.

God I love You

God, this is Gloria, your daughter.
Thank you for Jesus. I love you, Jesus.
Most of all, thank you, God for loving me so much.
There is no greater love than yours.
Your love keeps me when I can't seem to take care of myself.
Your love covers me as a blanket, warms me as the sun.
Your breath cools me when I need to be cool.
Your word is your eye that draws me to you.
Your voice is so sweet when it touches my heart. You are my every heartbeat.
Thank you, you carried me on your shoulders and when you let me down you then walked beside me and led me on the right path in my life.
Thank you for saving me, so I will be with you forever.
I love this life you have given me.
I can't live without you.

Be For Real – Where are all the Gentlemen?

Where are the Gentlemen?
I am not speaking for you to be condemned.
Where did they go? Were they here for a little while to show?
Where did they wonder off, and never come my way? They have me looking every day.
Where are the gentlemen, I say?
Where is the man to hold my hand, and walk with me in this land?
Where is the Gentleman that will understand and will lend me a helping hand?
The man that will tip his hat as I pass him by, that will make me smile and that isn't shy.
A Gentleman is one that cares, find one if you dare.
They used to be everywhere, they were here and they were there.
Where are all the Gentlemen?

They just can't be seen, are they hiding when we are walking and riding by?
Gentlemen would ask you for a date and would never be late.
Bring back the Gentlemen. Whoever took them away?
I will keep looking if it takes forever and a day.

When I did not know

Thank you God, when I did not know I was in your Bosom and you let me go you sent me down on earth through a thing called birth and I did not know.
I can say I was a gift to man and woman that they did not keep.
You gave me to my grandpa and my grandma and I did not know.
Thank you, God you kept me, allowed them to raise and love me, so I could see how much you loved me and I did not know.
God, you are more than the world to me, and when you let me go you knew all about me and more. You placed me in the good times, growing up I had no whines.
From being a baby, to a toddler, and being a child as we say, to a teen and through me being a woman, I have come a long way.
When I became something that I did not know.

The 12 days of Heaven (Can you Imagine Song)

1. Thank God for welcoming me home.
2. Shout all over God's Heaven.
3. Meet all my family and friends that made it in.
4. Calm myself down, I got overwhelmed.
5. Put on my long white robe.
6. Wear my golden crown.
7. Spread my wings and fly.
8. Sing and shout the victory.
9. I won't die no more.
10. I won't have no more sick days
11. Tell the Story of how I made it over.
12. Sit down with my Jesus for a while.

Thank You God for Making Me

Only you God could have made me.
You made me in the image of you.
I am the only one that the world can see.
There is not another one of me.

Thank you for making me Black.
I am of color and that's a fact.

I like how you formed me in my mother's womb.
You made me beautiful. No one will ever see how I became me.

Thank you, God for how you brought me through different stages in my life and now I am a woman.
Thank you, God you are amazing.

I love you, God for your wonderful book, the Bible.

For me to see and learn of you so I will know what it is for me to do and how to live for you.

I love this world you put me in. I know that it's not my home, sometimes I feel so alone. I am living my life unto you, God, I thank you.

I never received a gift like this.

Thank you God for Jesus.

I went down to the church one day, and I heard the preacher say God has given us a gift you know come receive it before you go. So, I went up to the altar, my heart and spirit I opened. I had to get my present that was waiting there for me, and when I got down on my knees and touched that precious gift I opened it. And when I did I felt a sudden shift. Out of that gift that I received that day, I saw a brand new way. When I got up on my feet, my heart and Spirit leaped. The Lord Jesus was my gift. Thank you, Jesus you came to earth and died just for me. Jesus is my Lord and my personal savior.

The Lord Gave Me

I have a family who I gave my love. Each one born was as lovely as a dove.

Four little girls I had first, then a little boy to make it worse. Six years later came one more boy, he helped the first boy and brought us joy.

Then two more girls the Lord gave to me. What a family I have now. They are sweet as can be, not one of them showed me the trouble that I would see.

Then all of a sudden the first five grew up, left me the last three gentle as a pup. Now the three little ones are getting out of the way fast. I am going to miss them when they are grown at last. Then there I will be just me and my past, happy as can be about the past. Wish that they had a dad. I tried like Hell to get them one, but failed.

I tried to give them a home that we could share. Wish that I could have given them the best of care.

Well, I have a family that I raised the best I could and when they are all grown and have a family of their own I hope they won't forget me their one and only mom.

Dear Jesus I Love You

Thank you for saving me, so that I may have everlasting life with you.
You say in your word that if I love you then I will keep your commandments.
Thank you, God for Jesus. Thank you, Jesus that you took my awful sins upon yourself so that I could become righteous through you. I will never be able to thank you enough for what you have done for me and are continuing to do for me in my life.
Thank you for a true man and woman and prophet that is called by your name to help build up my Faith so that I can know how to walk and live for you. Thank you for my road map to Heaven that you left for us to come home with you. The Holy Bible your inspired word that will never fail, which is Christ Jesus. Amen.

Lord show me Your Way - Song

Lord, you are my Savior, show me your way
Lord, you are my keeper, lead me day by day.
Lord, you are my helper, guide my steps, I pray.
Lord, you are my comforter, yes, Lord I say.
Lord, you are my peace, you are like honey on a cone, you are sweet.
Lord, you are everything to me, my bright and morning star.

Rain Down On Me – Song

Rain down on me, Lord
Down, down, down
Rain down on me, Lord
Rain down on me
Get me soaked and wet
Get me soaked and wet
Cause a move Lord
Cause a Move in me
Shake me loose, Lord
Shake me loose

Right Now Harvest Church – Examples
My Pastors.

Thank you, God for my Pastors that are called by your name.
As they follow in your footsteps, they really aren't the same.

They will show you who they stand for, just to meet them you will know the light that God has given them. The glow you see it comes from Him. They love you with the love of God. They care about your soul.

They preach to all the son of God who came to save us all. They always take you to the word, for God wants no man to be lost. They pray for your salvation, the precious gift from God. They welcome you with open hearts. The word of God they always tell for they are steadfast in him and in him they will not depart. So, if you haven't been born again and you would like an example, stop by come in, sit down just look and listen. God will get your attention.

They preach the word, they live the word and they live by the word. You see God in their praise and worship. You see that they are real.

So, one day if you might be searching to find the right place and time, just stop by Right Now Harvest Church, where you can receive a free meal, and drink the drink of life.

Through the Good and the Bad

I'm going to serve Him through the good and the bad.
I'm going to serve Him through the good and the bad.
I'm going to serve Him through the good and the bad.

I know that good will go on.
I know that the bad just won't last.
Sometimes I get so heavy laden
I am almost level with the ground

But I'm going to praise Him through the good and the bad, I know that good will go on and I know the bad can't last.

Troubles will come and troubles will go, but I'm going to praise Him through the good and the bad.

But there is one thing for sure my God is a good God and He won't fail. Yes, my God is a good God and he won't fail.

The New Life God's Gonna Give ME

The new life God gonna give me.
I will be new from head to toe and everyone will see.

God is gonna take me in the sky.
He will give me wings to fly.

God got for me one big meal and I won't need no diet pills.

He is gonna give me a new job to do and I will never get tired.
I will have a new family forever and ever.

God is gonna give to me a new voice and I will praise him with a new song.

I am gonna have new feet, and new legs.
I will have no more pain, no more sick days will I know, walking and talking I will go.

Gonna be with my Jesus forever more.
I will be with my Jesus, him I adore.
Thank you, God for saving my children.
God you are so good to me.

You came down to this earth so we might become the righteousness of God.
Your name is above all names in Heaven and earth.
I love you, Lord and I lift my voice to worship you.
Take heed Lord to what you hear, may it be a sweet, sweet sound in your ear.

Thank you, Jesus for saving me.
Thank you, Jesus for letting my light shine so that others may see you through me and see that you are for real.

The 12 Days of Christmas with Jesus

On the first day of Christmas
 Jesus gave to me a new life to serve him.
On the second day of Christmas
 Jesus gave to me a new church that he set me in.
On the third day of Christmas
 Jesus gave to me three preaching preachers.
On the fourth day of Christmas
 Jesus gave to me four people dancing.
On the fifth day of Christmas
 Jesus gave to me five voices singing.
On the sixth day of Christmas
 Jesus gave to me six children laughing.
On the seventh day of Christmas
 Jesus gave to me seven ushers coming.
On the eighth day of Christmas
Jesus gave me eight blessings with overflowing.
On the ninth day of Christmas
 Jesus gave to me nine ornaments for my tree.
On the tenth day of Christmas
 Jesus gave to me ten songs to sing.
On the eleventh day of Christmas

Jesus gave to me a brand new heart
On the twelfth day of Christmas
Jesus gave to me his Love & heavenly home.

A Mother's Christmas Wish – Nothing can Change what it is.

Merry Christmas to all of you. To my children, grands, and great-grands.

I wish you all in this Christmas season, will come together as one. Take time out to count your blessings. I am your mother, so count me. All of you came from me and I thank God for all of you. I know I am blessed and I have no regrets. Listen, my children, don't give me a deaf ear, we have been together for many a year and my wish is that you stop living without forgiveness and with fear. Yes, that is what you are doing. There are too many of you turning away from each other. It is passed time, it's time to wake up. Your heart's have grown cold and are beating very fast. So, whatever kind of mother you think I was, good or bad, put it behind you and stop thinking like fools. What I did and said, that's over and done. Stop dying and live because life goes on. I gave birth to you all and really eight wasn't enough. I love you all with all of my heart and soul. I kept you, raised you, and loved you all by myself and I did the best I knew how. So, my wish this Christmas is for you to search yourself. My children, stop what you are doing and start walking in forgiveness, then you will live in love and you all will be happy.

Author's Biography

Gloria J. Horton Malone was born in Athens Alabama, Lime Stone County. She was raised by her grandfather and step-grandmother. At the age of eleven she became a foster child. Being raised in the country gave her a great appreciation for God's Creation and the beautiful nature of his Glory.

Gloria loves to fish and remembers going with her grandmother when she was a young child. She would play with animals, bugs, worms, and she would always take time to smell the flowers.

Growing up she also loved going to church, learning about God and how much he loved her. Her grandmother was a God-fearing woman and she made sure Gloria was in church learning to trust in, and live for God.

Gloria believes that her love for God and his nature have kept her throughout her life.

She credits her faith for bringing her this far in life. Saying "I love God, my creator. His love is never ending."

www.ingramcontent.com/pod-product-compliance
Lightning Source LLC
Chambersburg PA
CBHW051714090426
42736CB00013B/2694